Prepare for Medicare

The Insider's Guide™

WORKBOOK

**YOUR COMPANION GUIDE
TO PREPARE FOR MEDICARE**

Matt Feret

INTRODUCTION

Welcome to the Prepare for Medicare workbook! This workbook is meant to work as an extension to the book, *Prepare for Medicare: The Insider's Guide to Buying Medicare Insurance*. This workbook does not contain all of the details covered in the book. However, it *can* be used as a stand-alone piece, which might also be helpful for financial planners or people assisting loved ones in making or reviewing their Medicare insurance choices.

This workbook can also serve as a very handy guide to keep healthcare, personal and financial information in one place for easy reference. Caring for parents or other loved ones can be difficult, especially when trying to track Medicare insurance information alongside other related items like:

— Financial advisor(s)

— CPA or tax professionals

— Medicare insurance agent

— Property and Casualty insurance agent

— Estate Planning contacts

— Banking information

— Life insurance policies with up-to-date beneficiaries

— Long-term care insurance polices

— Healthcare Power of Attorney

This workbook will also provide space to optionally note those items as well.

★ ★ ★ ★ ★

If you are brand new to Medicare, or even if you've been on Medicare for a while, you might want to consider filling out an Authorization Form to allow family or friends to call Medicare on your behalf. You must give prior permission, in writing, for someone to be given access to your personal health information. You can "revoke permission" or change the individual listed as authorized later if you like. It's just important to make sure you take care of this before it's needed. Find the authorization form by hitting the website at www.PrepareforMedicare.com/links or by typing this into your browser: https://bit.ly/3r8BTRQ

You should fill it out online, print it and mail it into the address at the bottom of the form. Alternatively, follow the directions at the top of the document and complete the Authorization form online by logging into www.MyMedicare.gov with valid credentials. Authorized Representatives can be added or updated under 'My Accounts'.

This workbook will guide you through:

1 Medicare basics, and (briefly) the *three* ways you can "consume" your Medicare benefits.

2 How to decide which of the three ways is right for you and how to purchase a Medicare insurance plan.

3 How to DIY or identify an expert Medicare insurance agent to help you.

4 What to do every October to make sure you're still in the best plan(s) that fit your healthcare, budget and lifestyle.

THIS WORKBOOK
COMES IN THREE SECTIONS

SECTION ONE: PREPARE INITIALLY

This section is meant for folks who are new to Medicare or are going to be eligible for Medicare soon. It's also very helpful for people who are helping loved ones or clients. It walks you through how to think about making Medicare insurance coverage choices and guides you towards which of the three Medicare insurance coverage options you can choose from.

There are *only three ways* to "consume" your Medicare benefits!

(I've **bolded** what you'll have to actually buy or purchase from a Medicare insurance company.)

OPTION 1: BARE-WITH-MEDICARE

OPTION 2: MEDICARE PART D + SUPPLEMENT

OPTION 3: MEDICARE PART C

There's always a debate: which option is "best?" There's no clear-cut answer as it's very individualized choice (as described in the book) but many people end up debating between Option 2 or Option 3. So, there's also a section to help you think through whether or not you should buy Option 3, Medicare Advantage plan or Option 2, Medicare Part D Prescription Drug Plan + Medicare Supplement plan.

SECTION TWO: PREPARE ANNUALLY

This is for folks currently on Medicare who have already have some sort of Medicare insurance coverage. This section walks you through what to do if you need to change your Medicare insurance coverage during the AEP that runs from October 15 through December 7th every year, or during the OEP (MAOEP) that runs from January 1 through March 31 each year. It also covers the ins-and-outs of changing from a Medicare Supplement plan to a Medicare Advantage plan and vice-versa. It helps outline what you should do each and every October to make sure you're still in the right plan for you and at the right price and benefits.

Regardless of whether or not you're brand-new to Medicare, or have been on Medicare for a while, it might be helpful to review both sections – there are nuggets of information that might refresh your memory or perspective!

SECTION THREE: PREPARE TO PURCHASE

This section runs you through the information valuable to consider and gather while you're making your Medicare insurance purchasing decisions. This section also addresses how to go about purchasing Medicare insurance from a Medicare insurance agent.

NOTES

_____

_____

_____

_____

_____

_____

_____

NOTES

MY PERSONAL
MEDICARE INFORMATION

MEDICARE HEALTH INSURANCE

Name/Nombre

Medicare Number/Número de Medicare

Entitled to/Con derecho a   Coverage starts/Cobertura empieza
HOSPITAL (PART A)
MEDICAL   (PART B)

MY INFORMATION

My Medicare Number : _____

Medicare Part A Eligibility Date: : _____

Medicare Part B Eligibility Date : _____

County : _____

Birthdate : _____

MY SPOUSE/PARTNER'S INFORMATION

My Medicare Number : _____

Medicare Part A Eligibility Date: : _____

Medicare Part B Eligibility Date : _____

County : _____

Birthdate : _____

MY HEALTHCARE INFORMATION

Having all of your healthcare information in one place is a handy way to keep track of what your costs are, where you get your prescription drugs from and what each prescription costs you.

It's also a great way to keep all of your doctors and other healthcare providers all in one place when you shop for Medicare insurance coverage or switching your coverage with or without the assistance of a Medicare insurance agent.

MY PRESCRIPTIONS

Prescription drug name: _____

Tier: _____

Dosage: _____

How often do you take a pill? _____

How often is this prescription refilled? _____

Quantity: _____

Filled at the pharmacy? yes ☐ no ☐

Filled by mail-order? yes ☐ no ☐

MY PRESCRIPTIONS

Prescription drug name: _____

Tier: _____

Dosage: _____

How often do you take a pill? _____

How often is this prescription refilled? _____

Quantity: _____

Filled at the pharmacy? yes ☐ no ☐

Filled by mail-order? yes ☐ no ☐

MY PRESCRIPTIONS

Prescription drug name: _____

Tier: _____

Dosage: _____

How often do you take a pill? _____

How often is this prescription refilled? _____

Quantity: _____

Filled at the pharmacy? yes ☐ no ☐

Filled by mail-order? yes ☐ no ☐

MY PRESCRIPTIONS

Prescription drug name: _____

Tier: _____

Dosage: _____

How often do you take a pill? _____

How often is this prescription refilled? _____

Quantity: _____

Filled at the pharmacy? yes ☐ no ☐

Filled by mail-order? yes ☐ no ☐

MY PRESCRIPTIONS

Prescription drug name: _____

Tier: _____

Dosage: _____

How often do you take a pill? _____

How often is this prescription refilled? _____

Quantity: _____

Filled at the pharmacy? yes ☐ no ☐

Filled by mail-order? yes ☐ no ☐

MY PRESCRIPTIONS

Prescription drug name: _____

Tier: _____

Dosage: _____

How often do you take a pill? _____

How often is this prescription refilled? _____

Quantity: _____

Filled at the pharmacy? yes ☐ no ☐

Filled by mail-order? yes ☐ no ☐

MY PRESCRIPTIONS

Prescription drug name: _____

Tier: _____

Dosage: _____

How often do you take a pill? _____

How often is this prescription refilled? _____

Quantity: _____

Filled at the pharmacy? yes ☐ no ☐

Filled by mail-order? yes ☐ no ☐

MY PRESCRIPTIONS

Prescription drug name: _____

Tier: _____

Dosage: _____

How often do you take a pill? _____

How often is this prescription refilled? _____

Quantity: _____

Filled at the pharmacy? yes ☐ no ☐

Filled by mail-order? yes ☐ no ☐

MY PRESCRIPTIONS

Prescription drug name: _____

Tier: _____

Dosage: _____

How often do you take a pill? _____

How often is this prescription refilled? _____

Quantity: _____

Filled at the pharmacy? yes ☐ no ☐

Filled by mail-order? yes ☐ no ☐

MY PRESCRIPTIONS

Prescription drug name: _____

Tier: _____

Dosage: _____

How often do you take a pill? _____

How often is this prescription refilled? _____

Quantity: _____

Filled at the pharmacy?   yes ☐   no ☐

Filled by mail-order?   yes ☐   no ☐

MY PRESCRIPTIONS

Prescription drug name: _____

Tier: _____

Dosage: _____

How often do you take a pill? _____

How often is this prescription refilled? _____

Quantity: _____

Filled at the pharmacy?   yes ☐   no ☐

Filled by mail-order?   yes ☐   no ☐

MY PRESCRIPTIONS

Prescription drug name: _____

Tier: _____

Dosage: _____

How often do you take a pill? _____

How often is this prescription refilled? _____

Quantity: _____

Filled at the pharmacy?   yes ☐   no ☐

Filled by mail-order?   yes ☐   no ☐

MY PREFERRED PHARMACY

Name : _____

Address : _____

Phone : _____

MY CHRONIC/PRE-EXISTING MEDICAL CONDITIONS

_____
_____
_____
_____
_____
_____
_____
_____
_____
_____
_____
_____
_____

I feel: (Circle one)

☺   ☺   ☹

healthy   mostly healthy   not very healthy

MY DOCTOR

Primary Care Physician : _____

Phone : _____

OTHER DOCTORS I USE

Physician : _____

Phone : _____

Physician : _____

Phone : _____

Physician : _____

Phone : _____

Physician : _____

Phone : _____

Physician : _____

Phone : _____

OTHER DOCTORS I USE

My dentist : _____

Phone : _____

My optometrist : _____

Phone : _____

My audiologist : _____

Phone : _____

My preferred hospital(s) : _____

Phone : _____

My preferred outpatient facilities : _____

Phone : _____

My preferred assisted living or long-term care facilities _____

Phone : _____

OTHER DOCTORS I USE (CONTINUED)

OTHER DOCTORS I USE (CONTINUED)

SECTION ONE: PREPARE INITIALLY

This section is meant for folks who are new to Medicare or are going to be eligible for Medicare soon.

WHAT IS MEDICARE?

Original Medicare is medical insurance for people over the age of sixty-five, and people under sixty-five with a long-term disability, or those who have certain disabilities like End-Stage Renal Disease (ESRD) or Amyotrophic Lateral Sclerosis (ALS), commonly known as Lou Gehrig's disease. Once you're eligible, there's no need to medically "qualify" for Medicare—you get it regardless of your current health. There are no health questions you need to answer to get Medicare. Once you have it, you cannot get kicked off of it for any medical condition or health-related reason. While there are certain limitations to care, and monthly premiums may differ from individual to individual, it does not "run out."

There are four parts of Medicare. Medicare Part A and Medicare Part B were the original choices rolled out in the 1960s. Thus, "Original Medicare" refers to Medicare Part A and Part B; Part C and Part D were added later.

 MEDICARE PART A: hospital insurance covers inpatient hospital care, skilled nursing facility, hospice, surgery, and some home health care.

 MEDICARE PART B: helps pay for services from doctors and other health care providers, outpatient care, lab tests, some home health care, and durable medical equipment.

Here's a list of what *isn't* covered under Original Medicare Part A and B:

1 Retail prescription drugs (covered under Part D)

2 Custodial care (help with bathing, dressing, using the bathroom, and eating)

3 Long-term care (nursing homes, retirement homes, and assisted living facilities)

4 Cosmetic Surgery

5 Most chiropractic services when not medically necessary

6 Routine dental and vision services

7 Most care while traveling outside the United States

 MEDICARE PART C: also known as Medicare Advantage. These are typically "combo" products of Medicare A, B, and D, although some *do not* include Part D. These are only sold by insurance companies.

Additional items Medicare Advantage insurance companies can include in their insurance coverage are:

Private hospital room or private nursing in the hospital

- Healthy food dollar amount allowances at grocery stores
- Adult Daycare visits and personal home helpers
- Lifestyle drugs, including erectile dysfunction prescriptions
- Air Conditioner allowances for people with COPD and asthma
- Transportation to doctor's appointments
- Nutritional programs, personal trainers, and access to spas
- Grocery delivery
- Flexible dollar amount allowances for healthcare-related items at select retailers (sometimes in the hundreds of dollars per year).
- Acupuncture and massage therapy
- Gym memberships or fitness classes
- Weight management programs
- Dental insurance & dentures
- Routine eye exams & glasses
- Routine hearing tests and hearing aids
- In-home safety assessments and services

MEDICARE PART D: helps pays for "retail" prescriptions, usually at your local pharmacy or via mail-order. Part D is used in two ways:

1. Embedded into certain Medicare Advantage plans (MAPD plans).

2. Offered as a stand-alone prescription drug insurance policy, used in conjunction with Original Medicare A and B medical coverage and oftentimes alongside a Medicare Supplement plan. Also commonly referred to as a Medicare Part D Prescription Drug plan, or a PDP.

Part D does not cover medical procedures—it only covers prescription drugs. These are only sold by insurance companies.

SIGNING UP FOR ORIGINAL MEDICARE, ENROLLMENT AND ELECTION PERIODS

1. INITIAL ENROLLMENT PERIOD (IEP)

To get Medicare Part A and Part B, there's something called an Initial Enrollment Period, or IEP, that lasts for seven full months. This time period starts three months prior to your sixty-fifth birthday. It includes the month in which you turn age sixty-five, and it then runs for an additional three months afterward. During this time period, you can sign up (or passively accept) Original Medicare Parts A and B and sign up for any of the three different coverage paths.

Most people get Medicare coverage automatically during this time, so there's nothing for you to do really but check your mailbox. These people include:

1. People turning sixty-five who are already receiving benefits from Social Security or the Railroad Retirement Board.

2. People under sixty-five with disabilities who have been receiving disability benefits for twenty-four months.

3. People living with ALS (Amyotrophic Lateral Sclerosis) receive coverage the month their Social Security benefits start kicking in.

However, scenarios do exist where you'll have to proactively sign up for Medicare:

1 People close to sixty-five and not receiving Social Security benefits.

2 People living in Puerto Rico—they'll have to sign up for Part B separately.

INITIAL COVERAGE ELECTION PERIOD (ICEP)

If you're deferring Part B for any reason, when you eventually do sign up for Medicare Part B, your election period code will most likely be the Initial Coverage Election Period or ICEP.

2. ANNUAL ELECTION PERIOD (AEP)

The AEP begins every year on October 15 and ends on December 7.

This is when you can change your Medicare Advantage plan or your Medicare Part D Prescription Drug Plan if you want. For instance, during the AEP, you can move from Original Medicare to Medicare Advantage or vice versa. You may also switch from one Medicare Advantage plan to another Medicare Advantage plan that may better suit your needs or your budget.

Likewise, you may also switch from one Medicare Part D Prescription Drug Plan to another, or you may join or leave a Medicare Part D plan altogether. Provided that you make any of these changes during the AEP, your new coverage will take effect on the following January 1, and your old one will immediately be dropped with no gap in coverage.

If you don't do anything or change anything, you just roll over and stay on the plan you have for the next year.

This does *not* apply to Medicare Supplement (Medigap) insurance. This period is *only* for changing Medicare Advantage plans and Medicare Part D Prescription Drug Plans.

3. OPEN ENROLLMENT PERIOD (OEP)

This is also known as the Medicare Advantage Open Enrollment Period (MAOEP)

The OEP runs from January 1st through March 31st every year. During this time, if you don't like the plan you bought, or something else changed between last year and this year, you can make a few changes.

During this time, you'll be able to:

1 Switch to a different Medicare Advantage plan.

2 Drop your Medicare Advantage plan and return to Original Medicare, Part A and Part B. This means if you do this, you can use the OEP to sign up for a stand-alone Medicare Part D Prescription Drug Plan (again, *only* if you return to Original Medicare and go Bare-with-Medicare).

3 Drop your stand-alone Medicare Part D Prescription Drug Plan. I can't think of a reason why you'd do that, but you can.

What *can't* you do during the OEP?

- Switch from Original Medicare to a Medicare Advantage plan.

- Switch from one stand-alone Medicare Part D Prescription Drug Plan to another.

4. SPECIAL ENROLLMENT PERIODS (SEP)

Simply put, a Special Enrollment Period (SEP) lets you make changes to your Medicare Advantage plan or Medicare Part D Prescription Drug Plan coverage outside of the regular enrollment periods listed above.

At last count, there are more than twenty-five types of SEPs. If you have one or think you might have one that applies to your situation, here's where a good independent Medicare insurance agent comes in handy. You can also call a Medicare insurance company and ask. I'd use an agent if you think you have some sort of event or extenuating circumstance outside of the IEP, AEP, and OEP that you need help with.

THE THREE MEDICARE PLAN COVERAGE OPTIONS

There are generally three Medicare plan coverage paths to choose from.

(I've **bolded** what you'll have to actually buy or purchase from a Medicare insurance company.)

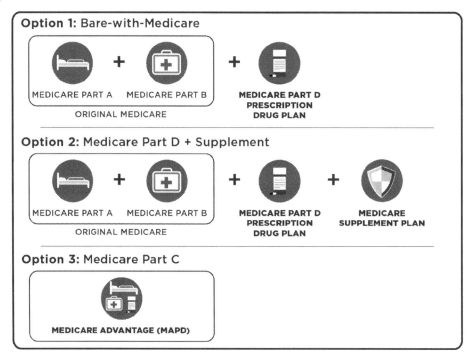

Most folks choose between Option 2 and Option 3, due to the coinsurance, deducible and copay "gaps" in Original Medicare coverage.

Which path should you choose? No answer is wrong, but you must choose one.

Here's another way to think about it. Medicare Supplements and Medicare Part D Prescription Drug Plans pay for items when you're sick, or they help you get better. When you go to the hospital, a Medicare Supplement helps pay the bill. When your doctor gives you a prescription, you use a Medicare Part D Prescription Drug Plan at your local pharmacy to fill that prescription.

Medicare Advantage plans do that as well, but because they can be built-in with so many additional options like gym memberships, OTC allowances, and healthy foods, you can use many Medicare Advantage plan features and benefits when you're *not* sick.

OPTION 1: BARE-WITH-MEDICARE

In this scenario, you use Original Medicare Plans A and B for your medical insurance coverage and simply buy a Medicare Part D Prescription Drug Plan to cover your prescription drug insurance. That's it. Simple. You're done. Original Medicare handles the majority of your healthcare needs, and you're looking at buying a Medicare Part D Prescription Drug Plan from one of many Mcdicare insurance companies for your prescription drug needs. It works this way just fine. People have been using Original Medicare for their medical coverage since Harry and Bess Truman (the first Medicare recipients). You'll have two cards in your wallet—your Original Medicare red, white, and blue card to use for medical needs, and a Medicare Part D Prescription Drug Plan card you'll use at your pharmacy. Expect to normally pay anywhere between $8-$60 per month for your Medicare Part D Prescription Drug Plan.

Unlike Original Medicare, which is administered by the federal government, Part D is administered and sold by insurance companies. There is no federal or public option. You can find a Medicare Part D Prescription Drug Plan through Medicare's website, but you buy it from an insurance company. You can also buy it straight from the insurance company's website, by calling them, or with the help of a Medicare insurance agent. If this is what you want to do, I recommend you simply use Medicare.gov to enroll in your Medicare Part D Prescription Drug Plan when you're able, and you're all set.

Using Original Medicare Parts A and B and buying a Medicare Part D Prescription Drug Plan is the most straightforward, easiest process that exists when it comes to consuming your Medicare benefits.

OPTION 1: PROS AND CONS

Simple. Lower premiums than Option #2. Easy to DIY. Likely the lowest cost for hospitalization when compared to Option 3, Medicare Advantage. No networks for medical coverage.

No MOOP, so financial exposure is technically unlimited. Twenty percent coinsurance for medical. Potential exposure to Medicare excess charges. Limited overseas travel coverage. Doesn't offer "extra" coverage that Medicare Advantage plans can offer. Deductibles and premiums go up every year. Preferred vs. non-preferred pharmacies might surprise you with higher costs.

OPTION 2: MEDICARE PART D + SUPPLEMENT

Under this scenario, you buy a Medicare Part D Prescription Drug Plan outlined in the prior section to cover your prescription drugs, keep Original Medicare, and also buy a Medicare Supplement plan to insure yourself for the portion of medical costs Original Medicare doesn't cover. Approximately 29% of the sixty-seven million people on Medicare use this option.

Medicare Supplement plans available for purchase today do *not* cover Medicare Part D prescription drugs, so if you go this route, you will have to buy two insurance policies—a Medicare Supplement policy from company 1, and a Medicare Part D Prescription Drug Plan from company 2. This also means you'll have to pay for two separate insurance policies. Sometimes company 1 and company 2 can be the same company—there's no harm in that. But, generally, these two types of insurance plans *don't coordinate*. In other words, they don't talk to each other, so there's no real advantage of bundling both together. This means you'll have three insurance cards in your wallet, your Original Medicare card, one for the Medicare Supplement plan you use for your medical needs and a Medicare Part D Prescription Drug Plan card you'll use at the pharmacy for your prescription drugs.

Medicare Supplement are also referred to as **Medigap Plans**. These can be compared to something like a pre-paid Medicare insurance plan. If you buy a Medicare Supplement Plan G, you're paying the insurance company a hefty premium every month to pay 100% of the bills after the Medicare Part B deductible. Once you've paid that deducible, generally that's it—you don't have to pay a penny more for any medical care for the rest of the year; the insurance company pays the rest. Medicare Supplements are as close to set-it-and-forget-it as you can possibly get in the Medicare insurance world.

Medicare Supplement plans have been around for a very long time but came under federal oversight in the early 1980s and have undergone several transformations since then. Today, Medicare supplement plans come in several flavors, which have letters attached to them. These are A, B, C, D, F, High-F, G, High-G, K, L, M, and N. There's also something called Medicare Select Plans, which are essentially Medicare Supplement plans with networks. I wouldn't pay much attention to those because they're pretty scarce, come with network restrictions, and not many folks buy them.

MEDIGAP PLAN COMPARISON CHART

Medigap Plan Benefits	Plan A	Plan B	Plan C	Plan D	Plan F	Plan G	Plan K	Plan L	Plan M	Plan N
Medicare Part A Coinsurance & Hospital Costs Up to an additional 365 days after Medicare benefits are used	100%	100%	100%	100%	100%	100%	100%	100%	100%	100%
Medicare Part B Coinsurance or Copayment	100%	100%	100%	100%	100%	100%	50%	75%	100%	100%***
Blood (First 3 Pints)	100%	100%	100%	100%	100%	100%	50%	75%	100%	100%
Part A Hospice Care Coinsurance or Copayment	100%	100%	100%	100%	100%	100%	50%	75%	100%	100%
Skilled Mursing Facility Coinsurance	X	X	100%	100%	100%	100%	50%	75%	100%	100%
Medicare Part A Deductible	X	100%	100%	100%	100%	100%	50%	75%	50%	100%
Medicare Part B Deductible	X	X	100%	X	100%	X	X	X	X	X
Medicare Part B Excess Charges	X	X	X	X	100%	100%	X	X	X	X
Foreign Travel Emergency up to plan limits	X	X	80%	80%	80%	80%	X	X	80%	80%

* Medicare Supplement Plan F and G are also offered as a high-deductible plans by some insurance companies in some states. If you choose this, no coverage begins until you pay the $2,370 deductible (2021).

** Out-of-Pocket Limit $6,220 $3,110

** Medicare Supplement Plan N pays 100% of the Part B coinsurance, except for a copay of up to $20 for some office visits and up to a $50 copay for ER visits that don't result in an inpatient ad mission.

SIMPLICITY – STANDARDIZED PLANS

All insurance companies offering Medicare Supplement coverage use the same letters. Each letter has a standard benefit, and they don't vary from company to company. This means, if you buy a Medicare Supplement plan G from United Healthcare, it's the same as buying a Medicare Supplement plan G from Mutual of Omaha or any other company. They're exactly the same except for the price. It pays to shop for the best price.

GUARANTEED RENEWABILITY

As long as you keep paying your monthly premium, the insurance company can't kick you off the plan, even if you get deathly ill.

BENEFITS DO NOT CHANGE

Unlike Medicare Advantage and Medicare Part D Prescription Drug plans, the benefits do not change every year.

NO NETWORKS

Any doctor, facility, or hospital that accepts Medicare assignment will take a Medicare Supplement anywhere in the country.

NO PROVIDER NETWORK HOOPS TO JUMP THROUGH

If Original Medicare says it's covered, then the Medicare Supplement insurance companies simply pay what's left over. There are rarely any questions. If Original Medicare pays your claim, your Medicare Supplement plan usually pays. Period.

NO REFERRALS REQUIRED

Unlike some Medicare Advantage plans (HMO plans, generally), you don't have to go to your primary care physician first before you get permission or a referral to see a specialist.

TRAVEL

Within the USA and its territories, there are no network restrictions. That means, if you live in Missouri and spend a lot of time with family in Illinois, you can go to doctors in either state, and the coverage will be the exact same. You don't even have to check with the insurance company.

If you have Medicare Supplement Plan C, D, F, G, M, or N, you even have some emergency coverage for overseas travel. However, it's limited to a $50,000-lifetime amount, and once you've been out of the US longer than sixty days, you're no longer covered by your Medicare supplement. There's also a $250 yearly deductible that you must meet before your plan kicks in, and then you'll have coinsurance to pay after the deductible up to a certain dollar amount, commonly $50,000. Just like in the US, your Medicare Supplement plan will only pay if the claims would normally be Medicare-approved. However, Original Medicare (Bare-with-Medicare) actually pays nothing for foreign travel.

PREDICTABLE SPENDING

When you buy a Medicare Supplement Plan G and pay your Part B deductible, you're done. You won't pay out of pocket for anything else that's Original Medicare-approved for the rest of the calendar year. Not true for Medicare Advantage plans, which have a dizzying array of deductibles, coinsurances, and copays.

NO ANNUAL REVIEW

Because Medicare Supplement plans are standardized, the benefits never change. Ever. If you buy a Plan G today, those benefits will be the same for the rest of your life. Thus, you don't have to do an annual review or worry about what's changing in your Medicare Supplement plan every year, like you do with Medicare Advantage.

LESS PAPERWORK, LESS HASSLE

If Original Medicare pays your medical claim, your Medicare Supplement plan works with your medical provider's billing office to send payment right to them, bypassing the need for you to get involved. Plan payments are straightforward; if Original Medicare paid, the Medicare Supplement insurance company pays what it should. Period.

MOVE TO A MEDICARE ADVANTAGE PLAN ANYTIME

You don't need to keep your Medicare Part D Prescription Drug Plan + Medicare Supplement if it gets too expensive or you just don't like it. You can move to a Medicare Advantage plan during any AEP (October 15-December 7 every year). But remember, be careful if you decide to do this. (See Chapter Two in the book for more on this topic).

DISCOUNT PROGRAMS AND SPECIAL BENEFITS

Some Medicare Supplement insurance companies offer premium discounts for spouses and partners buying together, gym memberships, and other items.

CONS:

PREMIUMS

A Medicare Supplement Plan G can easily cost you $150 per month when you're under seventy, and well over $200 when you're over seventy.

NO PRESCRIPTION DRUG COVERAGE

Don't forget, Medicare Supplement plans don't cover outpatient prescription drugs, so you'll have to buy a Medicare Part D Prescription Drug Plan, too. Those can cost anywhere between $8-$60 on top of the Medicare Supplement premium.

RISING PREMIUM PRICES AS YOU GET OLDER

Medicare Supplements premiums generally get more expensive the older you get.

Medicare Supplements often provide discounts for signing up at age sixty-five, or for signing up a spouse or partner at the same time (called household discounts) but cost more if you use tobacco. Some of those discounts go away after age sixty-five.

Medicare Supplement plan monthly premiums usually have rate increases every year, and not always centered around the beginning or the end of the year. Often, it's on your policy anniversary, which may not line up with Medicare's AEP for the Medicare Part D Prescription Drug Plan you have.

MEDICAL UNDERWRITING

If you're turning sixty-five or getting Medicare for the first time, it's extremely important to know there are only certain times you can buy a Medicare supplement without being asked health questions. If you've previously been or are very sick (cancer, heart attack, stroke, etc.) before you got Medicare and want to make sure you can get a Medicare Supplement plan with no health questions, *it is paramount you don't miss this window.*

Several states have exceptions to this. I cover these in the book.

LOOKBACK PERIODS

Depending on when you sign up, the insurance company might not treat a pre-existing condition for the first six months. Original Medicare will cover its portion, but the Medicare Supplement insurance plan may not cover what it was supposed to.

OPTION 3: MEDICARE PART C

In this scenario, you buy a Medicare Advantage plan that covers your medical costs as well as your Medicare Part D prescription drug coverage. Remember, these are Medicare Part C plans. These are combo plans—they cover the medical benefits of Original Medicare Parts A and B, as well as D. Approximately 35% of the sixty-seven million people on Medicare use this option. At a glance, it's easy to see why. Premiums for these range from $0 to over $100, but most people pay $0 to about $40 per month for these. It's a pretty compelling package to consider—you get Medicare Parts A, B, and D all in one package for a relatively low (or no) premium, hence its popularity.

These plans look sort of like traditional insurance you get from work, except, in most cases, they are far better. There are low copays for doctor visits, deductibles, coinsurance, and all of them must have MOOPs. Oftentimes, they do not have a deductible or coinsurances for many services. When they do, it's usually for using doctors who are not in their provider network, or for certain categories of prescription drugs.

Many Medicare Advantage plans offer additional benefits that Original Medicare does not. Examples of this are dental, vision, and hearing coverage, post-discharge meals, and free gym memberships.

Recall from earlier you cannot buy a federal or public-option Medicare Advantage plan. Medicare Advantage comes in a few shapes and sizes, but the vast majority of them are technically called Medicare Advantage-Prescription Drug plans. You might remember this acronym, pronounced M-A-P-D. There are MA-only plans out there, but those aren't the ones we're talking about here. Those are generally for veterans and folks on TRICARE.

When you buy one of these, it means, unlike the prior options, you don't flash your red, white, and blue Original Medicare card when you go to the doctor's office—you put it in your top drawer. Do not throw it away, but it won't work anymore. You get one card from the insurance company to use at the medical provider's office, the hospital, and at the pharmacy.

In order to buy a Medicare Advantage plan, you must have Original Medicare Parts A and B. You cannot simultaneously have a Medicare Supplement and a Medicare Advantage, nor can you simultaneously have a stand-alone Medicare Part D Prescription Drug Plan and an MAPD plan. Again, any combination of Option 1 or Option 2 from above will not work with an MAPD plan. To put it another way, you can have either Option 1 or Option 2, but neither of them if you choose Option 3, Medicare Advantage.

PROS 👍

All Medicare Advantage plans must have a MOOP (Maximum Out Of Pocket)!

Each Medicare Advantage plan must have an annual MOOP, or the bid from the insurance company won't be approved by Medicare. A MOOP is a limit of how much you'll pay – worst-case scenario – for medical coverage in a calendar year.

Remember, the MOOP is only for the medical portion, because the prescription drug benefit embedded in most Medicare Advantage plans has a separate schedule.

Medicare Advantage plans can be compared to something like a pay-as-you-go Medicare insurance plan. Instead of paying the insurance company upfront for near-100% coverage, you're paying them less and keeping that monthly premium in your pocket—ready and waiting for when you have to use it. Yes, Medicare Advantage plans come with lower monthly premiums, but you'll pay a larger percentage of your medical bills out of pocket when you use that insurance. Medicare Advantage plans charge you a portion of the bill nearly every time you see a doctor, get a test, have outpatient surgery, or go to the hospital. That's why the MOOP is so important; you want it to be as low as possible so that every year, you have a limit on your medical financial exposure.

👍 EXTRA COVERAGE NOT AVAILABLE IN ORIGINAL MEDICARE OR MEDICARE SUPPLEMENTS

Medicare Advantage plans are allowed to build into their plans and provide coverage for a whole array of additional health-related services not offered through Original Medicare. The most popular add-on benefits are dental insurance, vision, and hearing aid dollar allowances, free gym memberships, and dollar allowances for over-the-counter items at specific retail shops (like CVS or Walgreens) or via mail-order.

👍 LOW OR $0 PREMIUMS

There are many $0 plan offerings in the market today.

👍 CHRONIC CONDITION MANAGEMENT

Only Medicare Advantage plans have care management programs to specifically work with people with chronic conditions like high blood pressure, diabetes, heart failure, end-stage renal disease, rheumatoid arthritis, depression, and more. Treatment plans for these conditions usually involve a case manager, health coaching, medication therapy management, and more.

👍 NO HEALTH QUESTIONS

All Medicare Advantage plans must accept your application regardless of health status.

ONE INSURANCE PLAN, ONE INSURANCE COMPANY, ONE CARD

The vast majority of Medicare Advantage plans are MAPD plans, which, as previously noted, include medical and Part D prescription drug coverage. That means you only use one insurance card at the pharmacy, doctor's office, hospital, outpatient clinic—everywhere.

EXCESS CHARGES

If you have a PPO or an HMO-POS and go out of network and for some reason, that doctor doesn't accept Medicare Assignment, you may pay the full amount of the excess charges.

BENEFITS CHANGE EVERY YEAR

Since Medicare Advantage insurance companies must submit their bids to Medicare annually, that means the benefits of your Medicare Advantage plan can change every year. They can get better than the prior year. They can get worse than the prior year.

MONTHLY PREMIUMS CAN FLUCTUATE WILDLY

Some $0 plans go to $40 from one year to the next. I've seen those $40 plans go to $50 the next year, then back down to $40 the following, then to $20 the next, then right back to $40.

LACK OF PLAN CHOICES

Medicare Advantage plan offerings in rural counties can be drastically less—or even non-existent.

TOO MANY PLAN CHOICES

Sometimes, the opposite is true; as I've also covered, there are certain areas of the country that have over fifty Medicare Advantage plan options to choose from. How do you choose the "best" one?

YOUR PLAN CAN GET CANCELED!

Technically, they can't cancel you. But Medicare Advantage insurance companies can simply cancel the plan you're on at the end of the year, leaving you to scramble to find a new one by the deadline.

NETWORKS

All Medicare Advantage plans (except very rarely-offered PFFS, private-fee-for-service plans, and MSA plans) come with networks—HMO, HMO-POS, or PPO.

Provider directories are outdated or wrong – It's commonly known in the health insurance industry that printed network directories are outdated almost as they're being printed. This is because doctors, hospitals, and other medical providers are constantly being added or eliminated from networks.

HMOS USUALLY REQUIRE REFERRALS

In typical HMO plans, your primary care physician acts as your gatekeeper. That means they must refer you to specialists or other medical professionals; you can't just open your network directory and choose a specialist—you've got to get permission from your PCP first.

HIGH PPO OUT-OF-NETWORK COST-SHARING AND MOOPS

Many Medicare Advantage PPO plans place high deductibles on their medical benefits if you go out-of-network. Out-of-network MOOPs can be very high, especially in PPO plans.

MID-YEAR PROVIDER NETWORK CHANGES

If your doctor leaves or the insurance company cancels your doctor or hospital's contract in the middle of the year, you may have to find another provider in the network to treat you until you can switch Medicare Advantage plans during the AEP.

AFFORDABILITY AND YOUR BUDGET

OPTION 2: MEDICARE PART D + SUPPLEMENT

MEDICARE PART A   MEDICARE PART B
ORIGINAL MEDICARE

MEDICARE PART D PRESCRIPTION DRUG PLAN

MEDICARE SUPPLEMENT PLAN

If you choose this path, I'm going to recommend that you spend no more than 8% of your monthly gross income combined between your Medicare Supplement premium and your Medicare Part D premium. I've raised that to 8% because the most popular Medicare Supplements (Plan F, G, and N) have minimal deductibles and copays to contend with.

Maximum Monthly Medicare
Supplement Premium = _____

+ Medicare Part D Prescription
Drug Plan Premium = _____

Annual Total Premiums = _____

OPTION 3: MEDICARE PART C

I recommend that you do not spend more than 3% of your monthly gross income on a Medicare Advantage plan premium.

My recommendation is that you don't purchase a Medicare Advantage plan with an annual MOOP any higher than $4,000. If you ever have a horrible health year and hit your $4,000 MOOP (unlikely, but possible), that will essentially be 25% of the annual average Social Security benefit.

Maximum Monthly Medicare
Advantage Premium = _____

Annual Total Premiums = _____

AFFORDABILITY OVER TIME

How healthy are you? How long did your parents live? How long do you think you'll live? The other thing you'll want to consider around this topic is affordability over time. Since the introduction of Medicare Part D Prescription Drug Plans, the average monthly premiums for those policies have generally settled at around the $20-$25 mark. I wouldn't anticipate that to substantially increase above 1%-2% through inflation over the next twenty years.

Average Medicare Advantage plan insurance premiums seem to have actually leveled off or gone down since 2015. The average Medicare Advantage premium is $25 per month, although there are plenty of $0 options around.

However, the same can't be said for Medicare Supplement plans. Medicare Supplements generally increase in price the older you get while Medicare Advantage premiums are the same whether you're sixty-five or 105 years old. With Medicare advantage, the Medicare insurance company can change monthly premiums every calendar year for everyone on that particular plan.

I've demonstrated this in the chart below. What I've done is provided a real-life example of Option #2 – Original Medicare + Medicare Part D Prescription Drug Plan + Medicare Supplement.

I've taken a real-life example of a Medicare Supplement Plan G from a major insurance company and inserted their 2021 rates by age. I've even taken the liberty of showing the lower-priced female rates because rates for males are typically higher. I've also shown the preferred rates, not the standard rates.

Then, I've added in the Medicare Part D Prescription Drug Plan so we can see a total monthly bill for the Medicare Supplement *and* the Medicare Part D Prescription Drug Plan premiums over time. I've even assumed a 3% annual price increase for the Medicare Part D Prescription Drug Plan.

Then, I've compared that to a Medicare Advantage plan's premium over time.

Even though Medicare Advantage plan monthly premiums generally haven't increased in the last five years, let's assume those premiums go up 3% a year as well, just to be fair.

Take a look:

Assuming a $115 per month Medicare Supplement premium when you're sixty-five, plus a $20 per month Medicare Part D premium ($135/month) . . .

The results of comparing a Medicare Part D Prescription Drug Plan + Medicare Supplement to a Medicare Advantage plan by premium over time are pretty stunning.

In this example, if you buy a Medicare Supplement and a Medicare Part D Prescription Drug Plan when you turn sixty-five and keep it until you die at age ninety, you'll pay *$56,000 in insurance premiums.*

AGE	ANNUAL MEDICARE SUPPLEMENT PREMIUM	ANNUAL PART D PREMIUM	ANNUAL TOTAL	ANNUAL MAPD PREMIUM	ANNUAL TOTAL
65	$1,379	$240	$1,619	$300	$300
66	$1,389	$247	$1,636	$309	$309
67	$1,410	$255	$1,665	$318	$318
68	$1,439	$262	$1,701	$328	$328
69	$1,473	$270	$1,743	$338	$338
70	$1,507	$278	$1,785	$348	$348
71	$1,542	$287	$1,829	$358	$358
72	$1,578	$295	$1,873	$369	$369
73	$1,613	$304	$1,917	$380	$380
74	$1,651	$313	$1,964	$391	$391
75	$1,688	$323	$2,011	$403	$403
76	$1,727	$332	$2,059	$415	$415
77	$1,768	$342	$2,110	$428	$428
78	$1,808	$352	$2,160	$441	$441
79	$1,848	$363	$2,211	$454	$454
80	$1,890	$374	$2,264	$467	$467
81	$1,934	$385	$2,319	$481	$481
82	$1,976	$397	$2,373	$496	$496
83	$2,021	$409	$2,430	$511	$511
84	$2,064	$421	$2,485	$526	$526
85	$2,124	$433	$2,557	$542	$542
86	$2,169	$446	$2,615	$558	$558
87	$2,215	$460	$2,675	$575	$575
88	$2,261	$474	$2,735	$592	$592
89	$2,308	$488	$2,796	$610	$610
90	$2,353	$503	$2,856	$628	$628
TOTAL ANNUAL INSURANCE PREMIUMS PAID YEARS 65-90		$56,388			$5,868

The same scenario with a $25 per month premium Medicare Advantage plan? You've paid *only $5,800 in premiums over that same timeframe.*

Granted, Medicare Supplements provide more comprehensive medical payment coverage than Medicare Advantage plans do. The comparison above only measures annual insurance policy premiums.

But still, if you heed my advice and don't buy a Medicare Advantage plan with greater than a $4,000 MOOP, you could hit that catastrophic MOOP *level for thirteen of those twenty-five years* ($4,000 X 13 = $52,000) and still not have paid as much as just the Medicare Part D Prescription Drug Plan + Medicare Supplement premiums ($56,388). I'm not going out on a very long limb when I say it's impossible to hit a $4,000 MOOP thirteen years out of twenty-five and still be alive.

If they can afford it, many people like the simplicity and freedom Medicare Supplement plans provide. But examined over time, that freedom and simplicity certainly come at a cost. Can you afford that luxury? It's up to you. If you can't comfortably afford the option of Medicare Supplement + Medicare Part D Prescription Drug Plan, I'd urge you not to try.

NOW is the time to make your Medicare insurance coverage choice. So, which one will it be?

Circle ONE.

Option 1: Bare-with-Medicare

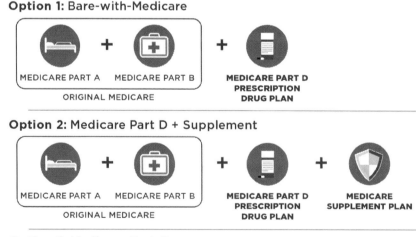

Option 2: Medicare Part D + Supplement

Option 3: Medicare Part C

OPTION 1: BARE-WITH-MEDICARE

If you choose this option, all you're doing is using Original Medicare to cover your medical healthcare and buying a Medicare Part D Prescription Drug Plan. The DIY process for buying a Medicare Part D Prescription Drug Plan through Medicare.gov is pretty easy.

You can use a fantastic independent Medicare insurance agent or Hybrid Agency to enroll in your Medicare Part D Prescription Drug Plan. However, I'd recommend using Medicare.gov exclusively to buy your Medicare Part D Prescription Drug Plan. In fact, Medicare.gov is a fantastic place to do this—probably even better, faster, and more convenient than using a Medicare insurance agent. It can be done in under an hour if you've got all of your pre-work checklists at the ready.

WHAT SHOULD YOU PRIORITIZE WHEN BUYING A MEDICARE PART D PRESCRIPTION DRUG PLAN?

When purchasing a Medicare Part D Prescription Drug Plan, keep these in mind:

1 Are all of your prescription drugs on the formulary? In other words, are they covered? The answer needs to be a yes to move forward.

yes ☐   no ☐

2 Where do your prescription drugs fall within the formulary? Tier 1 drugs are the least expensive for you; Tier 4+ are the most expensive. The more prescriptions you have that fall into the Tier 1 or Tier 2 category, the better.

_____

_____

_____

_____

3 Monthly Premium—the lower, the better.

Drug deducible—many companies have a deductible before any benefits kick in. Some only have deductibles on Tiers 3 and 4+ . You optimally want to buy one with no deductible, but the yearly drug and premium cost is more important.

yes ☐   no ☐

if yes, then how much and on what tiers? _____

4 Pharmacy—is your preferred pharmacy in the plan network? If not, and you don't have any particular allegiance to that pharmacy, are there others close by that you wouldn't mind using?

yes ☐   no ☐

if no, list alternate preferred pharmacy _____

5 Star Rating—needs to be 3.5 or higher for the Medicare Part D Prescription Drug Plan.

HERE'S HOW TO PURCHASE A MEDICARE PART D PRESCRIPTION DRUG PLAN ON MEDICARE.GOV, STEP-BY-STEP:

1 Navigate to Medicare.gov in your web browser.

2 Click "Find Health and Drug Plans."

3 Click "Continue Without Logging In."

⊘ You can create an account or log in if you already have one, but it isn't necessary.

4 Click the third option, "Drug Plan (Part D)."

5 Enter your ZIP code when prompted. Validate the county you live in if asked.

6 Click the last option, "I don't get help from any of these programs," then click Next.

7 Click yes when asked, "Do you want to see your drug costs when you compare plans?"

8 Click one of the three options that apply to you when asked, "How do you normally fill your prescriptions?" I would suggest using monthly as the option for viewing ease. Click Next.

9 In the next section, "Add prescription drug," enter in all of your prescriptions, including dosages and frequency. Reference your worksheet if you've filled it out.

10 When you're done adding in all of your prescriptions, click "Done Adding Drugs."

11 The next screen asks you to find your pharmacy. Search for your preferred pharmacy by name—or there's a helpful map on the page to use. You can enter up to five, but I'm guessing you probably only use one. Click "Done" at the lower right-hand part of the page when you're finished entering data.

What pops up are all of your Medicare Part D Prescription Drug Plan options. The screen will default to being sorted by "Lowest Drug + Premium Cost." That's a good way to sort your results. If you want to find plans without deductibles, you can do that by clicking the drop-down in the upper-right corner of the screen and selecting "Lowest yearly drug deductible." If you simply want to sort by the lowest monthly premium, you can do that too.

Whichever of the three sorting mechanisms you choose, I'd focus on the top three results. Give them a quick glance to make sure each of them is rated three and a half stars or above; I'd recommend you never consider anything under three stars. If the plan is flagged "Plan too new to be measured," that's okay, but realize it's a brand-new Medicare Part D Prescription Drug Plan.

The next step can be as simple or as complicated as you want to make it. You can compare up to three Medicare Part D Prescription Drug Plans side-by-side. Or you can just pick the top result and roll with it.

Either way, when you're ready to enroll, you just click, "Enroll." This will take you to a screen where you'll have to confirm your enrollment period. If you need a refresher, reference your checklist or workbook, or go back to Chapter Two and confirm that you're using the right enrollment period.

Once you've chosen your election period, click "Next."

This starts a seven-step process.

Step 1 of 7: Enter your Medicare number, which can be found on your red, white, and blue Medicare card. Click "I've read and understand the contents of this page," and click Next.

Step 2 of 7: Fill out your name, DOB, sex, and phone number. Make sure your name is the same as what's on your Medicare card. Click Next.

Step 3 of 7: Enter your address. Make sure it matches the one on your driver's license. Click Next.

Step 4 of 7: The next section asks several questions about any other drug coverage you have, whether or not you work, and whether or not you want your Medicare insurance plan documents physically mailed to you or just sent to your email. When you're done filling this section out, click Next.

Step 5 of 7: This section asks if you want to have the monthly premiums deducted from your Social Security or Railroad Retirement Board (RRB) benefits. You can choose this one (the easiest option, in my opinion), or you can elect to pay your plan directly. Be forewarned, sometimes it takes several months for Medicare, the Medicare insurance company, and Social Security to catch up and synchronize the billing. If you don't want that potential hassle, select Auto Bill Pay.

Step 6 of 7: This section is the legalese asking you to confirm what you've previously entered. Fill it out and click Next.

Step 7 of 7: This is the confirmation screen.

You're done! You've just signed up for a Medicare Part D Prescription Drug Plan.

WHAT HAPPENS NEXT?

You'll receive your Medicare Part D Prescription Drug Plan card in the mail generally within two weeks. You'll also get information in the mail unless you elected to receive plan documents via email. If you've messed anything up in the application process, the Medicare insurance company will reach out to you. It's important that you respond to them as quickly as possible.

OPTION 2: MEDICARE PART D + SUPPLEMENT

If you choose this option, you're using Original Medicare to cover your medical healthcare, buying a Medicare Part D Prescription Drug Plan and a Medicare Supplement plan. There are two steps to this process.

Step 1: Follow the DIY process above to buy your Medicare Part D Prescription Drug Plan, or use a Medicare insurance agent.

Step 2: Use a Medicare insurance agent or Hybrid Agency to buy your Medicare Supplement plan.

You can certainly DIY your own Medicare Supplement purchase. Doing research online for Medicare Supplements is not easy, and Medicare.gov's website for Medicare Supplements leaves much to be desired. Here's the link if you're interested: https://www.medicare.gov/medigap-supplemental-insurance-plans/

The site will allow you to enter your ZIP code, age, sex and tobacco status. When you do, it'll pop up a list of all the Medicare Supplement insurance companies selling Medicare Supplement insurance in your area. The rest of the legwork is up to you. If you choose to DIY instead of use a local independent Medicare insurance agent or online Hybrid Agency, you'll have to research each individual company's website on your own to compare plans available and pricing. It's not impossible, but it's tedious and will take several hours.

This is why I recommend using an independent Medicare insurance agent to buy your Medicare Supplement policy, or an online Hybrid Agency.

You can buy a Medicare Supplement plan on any number of the Hybrid Agencies I list on the website at PrepareforMedicare.com/links. However, as of this writing, many of those websites only let you get a step or two into the research before asking you for either more personal information or trying to get you to call their toll-free number, so please be aware you may not be able to see all your options online. You may have to interact with a telephone sales representative.

Alternatively, find a good local Medicare insurance agent in your area.

HOW SHOULD YOU PRIORITIZE BUYING A MEDICARE SUPPLEMENT PLAN?

I'd recommend prioritizing your shopping and buying around the following items from most important to least important.

1. Buy the most comprehensive Medicare Supplement plan you can. If you were eligible for Medicare before January 1, 2020, that's Plan F, followed by Plan C. If you weren't, those are no longer available. That means Plan G is the most comprehensive, followed by Plan N.

2. Premium—the lower, the better. Don't be fooled by introductory rates—look at the premiums over time.

3. Medicare star ratings don't apply to Medicare Supplement plans. Therefore, it's best to check the AM Best financial ratings of the Medicare Supplement companies you're considering (AM Best is a financial rating service). Most of the brand-name Medicare insurance companies you probably already recognize have high ratings, but if you're considering a smaller, lesser-known company, I'd check the ratings.

ELIGIBILITY: ARE YOU ELIGIBLE TO BUY A MEDICARE SUPPLEMENT PLAN?

Medicare Supplements are not like Medicare Advantage or Medicare Part D Prescription Drug cards. Those two plan types must accept you at certain times of the year no matter your health status. Medicare Supplement insurance companies largely do not have to accept you outside of your initial Medicare Supplement (Medigap) Open Enrollment Period, unless you answer health questions. This is generally when you turn 65.

That's not to say there aren't specific state rules that override that. There are Guarantee-Issue Medicare Supplement policies available, but the rules, number of plans available and prices vary wildly from state to state, even county to county. This is where a local expert independent Medicare insurance agent comes in very handy. They'll know the specific rules where you live and can save you literally hours of research.

1. Will you be enrolled in Medicare Parts A and B at the time your coverage begins? (Must be a yes)

yes ☐   no ☐

2 Are you a resident of the state in which you are applying for coverage? (Must be a yes)

yes ☐   no ☐

3 Have you had major health issues in the past?

yes ☐   no ☐

If you have that open window coming up because you're turning sixty-five or retiring and have had major illnesses or surgery in your pre-retirement life, please look very long and hard at buying a Medicare Supplement if you can afford one. We all know cancer can come back. We all know heart problems don't normally just go away. If you don't get it during this open window, you most likely won't be able to get it in the future.

4 Are you turning sixty-five or getting Medicare for the first time?

yes ☐   no ☐

If you're turning sixty-five or getting Medicare for the first time, it's extremely important to know there are only certain times you can buy a Medicare supplement without being asked health questions. If you buy a Medicare Supplement within the first six months of getting Medicare Part B, the insurance company has to accept you. *This is called the one-time Medicare Supplement (Medigap) Open Enrollment Period.* If you don't sign up for a Medicare Supplement plan within this timeframe, you will probably have to answer health questions and could be denied coverage. If you've previously been or are very sick (cancer, heart attack, stroke, etc.) before you got Medicare and want to make sure you can get a Medicare Supplement plan with no health questions, *it is paramount you don't miss this window.*

✅ Several states have exceptions to this. In California, you can switch your Medicare Supplement plans between carriers (as long as it's not an upgrade) every year in the sixty days following your birthday with no medical underwriting. In Oregon, you have thirty days. In Missouri, you can switch within sixty days of your anniversary date of your initial effective date into a Medicare Supplement plan. Washington, New York, Connecticut, Minnesota, and Wisconsin also have special rules that may allow you to switch.

5 Are you switching from a Medicare Advantage plan to a Medicare Supplement plan for the first time?

yes ☐   no ☐

BE CAREFUL.

Depending upon the rules of your particular state, you may have to go through medical underwriting to purchase a Medicare Supplement plan outside of a special window when you turn sixty-five. Medicare Supplement plans are *not* like Original Medicare Parts A and B, Medicare Part D, or Medicare Part C (Medicare Advantage plans) in that Medicare Supplement insurance companies *can* deny you coverage based on your health.

A Medicare Supplement policy is a separate policy from Original Medicare Parts A and B. Medicare Supplements are offered by Medicare Supplement insurance companies. These companies *can* deny you coverage or, at the very least, accept you but charge you a much higher premium. If you get denied coverage for a Medicare Supplement plan, you'll *only* have Original Medicare Parts A and B and a Medicare Part D Prescription Drug plan to fall back on, until the AEP (October 15-December 7th), when you can enroll in a Medicare Advantage plan once again. My advice is that if you want to go that way, you've got to apply and receive your acceptance or denial from the Medicare Supplement insurance company *before* you apply for Part D and drop your Medicare Advantage plan.

If you have missed that window, even if you're on a Medicare Advantage plan and want to switch to a Medicare Supplement, you'll most likely have to answer these health questions. If you're healthy, it may not be an issue, but logic dictates the older you are, the more likely you are to develop health problems.

Each Medicare Supplement insurance company has different rules and different medical questions. However, there are certain "kick-out" questions the majority of companies have that, if you answer yes to, automatically decline you. These generally have to do with whether or not you've been diagnosed or treated for any of the following conditions:

☐ Heart attack and other heart conditions

☐ Stroke

☐ Diabetes

☐ Lung disorders

☐ Prostate Cancer

☐ Osteoporosis, arthritis, or other conditions that restrict mobility

Never, ever cancel an existing Medicare Supplement policy without first confirming that a new Medicare Supplement policy has been issued or, if you're moving to a Medicare Advantage plan, confirming the new plan is in place. If you cancel your Medicare Supplement plan too early, they don't have to take you back.

MEDIGAP PLAN COMPARISON CHART

Medigap Plan Benefits	Plan A	Plan B	Plan C	Plan D	Plan F	Plan G	Plan K	Plan L	Plan M	Plan N
Medicare Part A Coinsurance & Hospital Costs Up to an additional 365 days after Medicare benefits are used	100%	100%	100%	100%	100%	100%	100%	100%	100%	100%
Medicare Part B Coinsurance or Copayment	100%	100%	100%	100%	100%	100%	50%	75%	100%	100%***
Blood (First 3 Pints)	100%	100%	100%	100%	100%	100%	50%	75%	100%	100%
Part A Hospice Care Coinsurance or Copayment	100%	100%	100%	100%	100%	100%	50%	75%	100%	100%
Skilled Nursing Facility Coinsurance	X	X	100%	100%	100%	100%	50%	75%	100%	100%
Medicare Part A Deductible	X	100%	100%	100%	100%	100%	50%	75%	50%	100%
Medicare Part B Deductible	X	X	100%	X	100%	X	X	X	X	X
Medicare Part B Excess Charges	X	X	X	X	100%	100%	X	X	X	X
Foreign Travel Emergency up to plan limits	X	X	80%	80%	80%	80%	X	X	80%	80%

* Medicare Supplement Plan F and G are also offered as a high-deductible plans by some insurance companies in some states. If you choose this, no coverage begins until you pay the $2,370 deductible (2021).

** Out-of-Pocket Limit $6,220 $3,110

** Medicare Supplement Plan N pays 100% of the Part B coinsurance, except for a copay of up to $20 for some office visits and up to a $50 copay for ER visits that don't result in an inpatient ad mission.

WHAT HAPPENS NEXT?

After you purchase your Medicare Supplement policy, you'll generally get confirmation letters or emails confirming receipt of your application. You will also get a follow-up call from the insurance company if they need to validate any information you provided on the application.

Expect to get your ID cards in the mail within fourteen days. Since you bought the policy through an independent Medicare Agent or Hybrid Agency, you may also receive follow-up correspondence from the agency.

OPTION 3: MEDICARE PART C

MEDICARE ADVANTAGE (MAPD)

If you choose this option, you're using a Medicare Advantage plan with Medicare Part D benefits embedded into the plan. This is also known as an MAPD plan and covers your medical and prescription drug coverage.

Here you have two DIY options to choose from when buying a Medicare Advantage plan. For the first DIY option, you can use Medicare.gov to narrow down your top three choices, then move over to the Medicare insurance company websites to finish your research and buy the policy. For the second DIY option, you can use a Hybrid Agency website to buy your Medicare Advantage plan.

I'd frankly recommend you do not try to DIY this – it's certainly possible but will likely take several hours of website browsing. My advice would be this: do your research on Medicare.gov, narrow down your top three Medicare Advantage plan choices, then reach out to those Medicare insurance companies and have them send one of their independent Medicare insurance agents to meet you at your home or preferred location.

HOW SHOULD YOU PRIORITIZE BUYING A MEDICARE ADVANTAGE PLAN

Premium per month :

HMO or PPO :

MOOP

Inpatient Hospital Benefit

Primary Care Physician Copay

Specialist Copay

Outpatient Benefit

Diagnostic procedure costs:

Medicare star rating

Dental Allowance

Vision Allowance

Hearing Allowance

Gym Membership

Other benefits:

Prescription Drug Benefits

Hearing Allowance :

Gym Membership :

Other benefits :

Prescription Drug Benefits :

Tier 1 Copay :

Tier 2 Copay :

Tier 3 Copay :

Tier 4 Copay :

Tier 5 Copay :

Tier 6 Copay :

Drug Deductible?

HOW SHOULD YOU PRIORITIZE?

When purchasing a Medicare Advantage plan, keep these in mind:

1. Are your doctors in the insurance company's provider network? Is your preferred hospital in the insurance company's provider network? For doctors you see often, it's best to actually call their offices to double-check. If not, find a plan that has them in the network.

   yes ☐   no ☐

2. Monthly premium—the lower, the better, but don't let a $0 plan premium automatically sway you.

3. Primary care and specialist doctor copays – the lower, the better.

4. Prescription drug coverage – Are all of your prescription drugs on the formulary? In other words, are they covered? The answer needs to be a yes to move forward.

   yes ☐   no ☐

5. Where do your prescription drugs fall within the formulary? Tier 1 drugs are the least expensive for you, Tier 4 are the most expensive. The more prescriptions you have that fall into the Tier 1 or Tier 2 category, the better.

   yes ☐   no ☐

6. Prescription drug copays – the lower, the better..

7. Avoid deductibles on prescription drug coverage. Many companies have a deductible before any benefits kick in. Some only have deductibles on Tiers 3 and 4. You optimally want to buy one with no deductible.

8. MOOP – try to keep it under $4,000 per year.

9. Avoid any deductibles on medical coverage.

10. Inpatient hospitalization coverage—the lowest daily copays, for the fewest number of days is the best

11. Outpatient costs.

12. Diagnostic procedure costs – Lab, X-rays, etc.

13. "Extra" benefits (dental, vision, hearing, etc.) Dental allowance should be at least $1,000 per year.

14. Star Rating needs to be 3.5 or higher.

Author's note: In all cases, you're going to want to **be comfortable with the reputation and confident in the brand of the Medicare insurance company you're selecting or considering.** As you've seen throughout the book, there are only a handful of big-brand Medicare insurance companies that have hundreds of thousands of customers. That's not to say you have to buy from a big-brand Medicare insurance company, but I do urge you to do some research on their websites, ask friends, family, and Medicare insurance agents how they feel about their customer service and stability. You can also take them for a test drive. Call the companies you're considering and do some shopping. Ask questions. Ask what plans are available and how they treat their customers. You can find out a lot just by talking with phone representatives, Medicare insurance agents, family and friends.

Sample questions you might ask: Have you used customer service and was it good? Did you wait on hold for a long time? Bad sign. Positive or negative experience? Did they fix your problem with only one phone call? Were they quick? Did you get transferred around multiple times? When you signed up for your Medicare insurance plan, did you get a welcome call? Was the provider directory information accurate and up to date? Did your doctors or pharmacist tell you they didn't accept the plan, even thought they were listed in the directories. Do the monthly premiums change much, year-to-year? Have the plan benefits gone down or up over the last few years?

WHAT HAPPENS NEXT?

That's it! You're all done! Well, almost. If you've done everything correctly, you can expect your ID cards and other plan documents in the mail. If you messed something up on the application, expect the insurance agency to reach out to you. Or expect the Medicare insurance company to reach out to you.

Buying a Medicare Part D Prescription Drug Plan on Medicare.gov by yourself is pretty darn easy. (It's the easiest the DIY gets.) Buying a Medicare Supplement online is probably the next easiest because there are fewer offerings. Buying a Medicare Advantage plan gets insanely complex and difficult without expert advice.

If you decide to DIY, fantastic! But know that the vast majority of people end up asking for professional help in making this decision and enrolling in Medicare insurance plans. **If you're feeling overwhelmed or unsure, engaging an expert Medicare insurance professional is most likely the best move and one I wholeheartedly encourage you to consider.**

PURCHASING DECISION

COST

What's my monthly premium?

How much will my prescription drugs cost?

How much will it cost me to go to the doctor or the hospital?

What's my MOOP?

COVERAGE

Are my over-the-counter supplements, hearing aids, vision, and dental needs covered?

Other extra benefits?

Do I get a free gym membership with the insurance policy?

Can I use my insurance plan benefits when I travel?

CHOICE

Can I see my doctor(s)? How much will that cost me?

Can I see a large number of doctors? (Is the network large?)

Can I see any doctor that accepts Medicare?

Are my prescription drugs covered?

CONFIDENCE

Do I know the insurance company? Is it a brand I can trust?

SECTION ONE NOTES

SECTION ONE NOTES

SECTION TWO: PREPARE ANNUALLY

Every year, Medicare insurance companies change their Medicare Advantage and Medicare Part D Prescription Drug Plan benefits. Even if you stay on the plan you had the previous year, something usually changes from year to year. I've never seen a Medicare Advantage plan that did *not* change at least *something* from one year to the next. The same goes for Medicare Part D Prescription Drug Plans. Almost every plan makes some changes for the new year, so the costs and benefits in place on December 31 may be very different on January 1. Some of those changes can throw you for a loop if you're not aware of them or you're not prepared.

By September 30 of each year, your Medicare insurance company is required to send an outline of the changes to your plan for the following year. It's called an Annual Notification of Change or, ANOC. They usually give you *fifteen days to review what's in it* before the AEP begins on October 15. If you don't read your ANOC before then, you won't know what changes are being made to your plan until they go into effect on January 1.

Immediately go to the section entitled, ***Summary of Important Costs.*** It should be right up front, either page two or three. This section will give you a brief overview of what the Medicare insurance company considers *important*. It's good as a summary, but *you might have to dig a bit deeper into the document to see everything that's going on.*

For Medicare Part D Prescription Drug Plans, here's what to check (in this order):

1 Monthly premium. Did it go up?

yes ☐   no ☐

2 Did any prescription drug deductibles get introduced or increase?

yes ☐   no ☐

3 Check the formulary—did any prescription drugs you take get taken off the formulary or get bumped into a different (more expensive) tier?

yes ☐   no ☐

4 Check your copays for Tiers 1-4+. Did they get more expensive?

yes ☐   no ☐

1 Scan it for anything announcing that the pharmacy networks have changed—did they drop your preferred neighborhood pharmacy?

yes ☐   no ☐

If *any* of the answers to those five questions are yes, it's time to shop!

For Medicare Advantage Plans, here's what to check (in this order):

1 Monthly plan premium. Did it go up?

yes ☐   no ☐

2 MOOP—Did it go up or get worse? Is it over $4,000 per year?

yes ☐   no ☐

3 Doctor's office visit costs. Did the copays go up significantly?

yes ☐   no ☐

4 Inpatient hospital stay costs. Did they go up substantially?

yes ☐   no ☐

5 Did the potential costs for Outpatient procedures go up?

yes ☐   no ☐

6 Part B Drugs—did the benefits get worse?

yes ☐   no ☐

7 Did any prescription drug deductibles get introduced or increase?

yes ☐   no ☐

8 Check the formulary—did any prescription drugs you take get taken off of the formulary or get bumped into a different (more expensive) tier?

yes ☐   no ☐

9 Check your copays for Tiers 1-4+. Did they get more expensive?

yes ☐   no ☐

10 Scan it for anything announcing the pharmacy networks have changed—did they drop your preferred neighborhood pharmacy?

yes ☐   no ☐

11 Look for changes to your additional benefits, like dental, vision, and hearing. Any major? Any negative changes?

yes ☐   no ☐

Since there are so many categories, you have to consider their costs. I'd stick to the following: if the answer to 50% of those questions I listed here is yes, then it's time to shop. The exception to this rule is the MOOP. If the MOOP rose significantly or went over $4,000 a year, it's time to shop!

SWITCHING BETWEEN MEDICARE ADVANTAGE AND MEDICARE SUPPLEMENT

Want to drop your Option 2: Medicare Part D Prescription Drug Plan + Medicare Supplement and go to an all-in-one Medicare Advantage plan during the AEP between October 15 and December 7 of each year?

No problem!

Want to switch back later? Potentially *big* problem!

You can do this *only once*, and you can only do this within twelve months of such a switch, and you'll have to use a Special Enrollment exception to do it. This is called your "Trial Right" period. If you miss the window, you'll most likely be asked health questions and possibly be denied coverage if you want to re-sign up for a Medicare Supplement plan. Just like above, several states may have their own special rules. Again, I'd recommend not doing this until you talk to a representative from a Medicare Supplement insurance company or a Medicare insurance agent to help guide you through the process. Plan ahead—don't wait until the AEP starts and decide you want to do this. If you do this, you must call and cancel your Medicare Supplement yourself; the Medicare Advantage company won't do it for you.

It's tempting to think you can enroll in a Medicare Advantage plan when you're sixty-five and keep it for a few years *then* switch to a Medicare Supplement when you get sick and start to rack up medical bills. Of course, everyone wants the most comprehensive medical insurance coverage when they're sick, but it doesn't work that way. That's why you need to not only think about today but also *tomorrow*. **If you want to buy a Medicare Supplement when you're already sick, odds are, you'll be denied coverage.** Outside of some state rules and Guaranteed-Issue Medicare Supplement policies, the only exceptions to this are:

1 If you sign up for a Medicare Advantage plan at sixty-five (or when you first get Part B if you've worked past sixty-five) and want to switch to a Medicare Supplement plan within the first twelve months. You can do this using your "Trial Right" Special Election Period, but it has to be within the first twelve months of having that Medicare Advantage plan

2 If you had a Medicare Supplement plan, *then* switched to a Medicare Advantage plan and want to switch *back* to a Medicare Supplement plan. You can also do this using your "Trial Right" Special Election Period, but it has to be within the first twelve months of having that Medicare Advantage plan.

3 State-specific Guarantee Issue rules and certain Guarantee Issue Medicare Supplement plans.

1. ANNUAL ELECTION PERIOD (AEP)

The AEP begins every year on October 15 and ends on December 7.

This is when you can change your Medicare Advantage plan or your Medicare Part D Prescription Drug Plan if you want. For instance, during the AEP, you can move from Original Medicare to Medicare Advantage or vice versa. You may also switch from one Medicare Advantage plan to another Medicare Advantage plan that may better suit your needs or your budget.

Likewise, you may also switch from one Medicare Part D Prescription Drug Plan to another, or you may join or leave a Medicare Part D plan altogether. Provided that you make any of these changes during the AEP, your new coverage will take effect on the following January 1, and your old one will immediately be dropped with no gap in coverage.

If you don't do anything or change anything, you just roll over and stay on the plan you have for the next year.

This does *not* apply to Medicare Supplement (Medigap) insurance. This period is *only* for changing Medicare Advantage Plans and Medicare Part D Prescription Drug Plans.

2. OPEN ENROLLMENT PERIOD (OEP)

Although the Annual Election Period (AEP) ends on December 7 every year, that does not necessarily mean that you're completely out of luck if you still want to make a change after December 7. With the AEP occurring around the holidays, it's no wonder some folks simply miss it. During the Medicare Open Enrollment Period (OEP), some avenues could still allow you to make changes to your Medicare coverage without penalty and without having to wait until the AEP next year.

It's also known as the Medicare Advantage Open Enrollment Period (MAOEP)

The OEP runs from January 1st through March 31st every year. During this time, if you don't like the plan you bought, or something else changed between last year and this year, you can make a few changes.

During this time, you'll be able to:

1 Switch to a different Medicare Advantage plan

2 Drop your Medicare Advantage plan and return to Original Medicare, Part A and Part B. This means if you do this, you can use the OEP to sign up for a stand-alone Medicare Part D Prescription Drug Plan (again, *only* if you return to Original Medicare).

3 Drop your stand-alone Medicare Part D Prescription Drug Plan. I can't think of a reason why you'd do that, but you can.

What *can't* you do during the OEP?

⊗ Switch from Original Medicare to a Medicare Advantage Plan.

⊗ Switch from one stand-alone Medicare Part D Prescription Drug Plan to another.

If you decide to drop your Medicare Advantage plan and buy a Medicare Part D Prescription Drug plan during the OEP, you'll be bumped off of your Medicare Advantage plan and default back to Original Medicare A and B for your medical insurance coverage.

If you leave a Medicare Advantage plan during the Medicare Open Enrollment Period, your current Medicare Advantage coverage will remain in force until the end of the current month. Your new coverage will then take effect on the first day of the following month.

Please note, you can only make a change *one time* during the OEP. In other words, once you have made a change to your Medicare coverage using your OEP, that's it for the year. You may not go back in during this same time frame and make more changes.

MOVING FROM MEDICARE ADVANTAGE TO MEDICARE SUPPLEMENT PLANS AFTER THE 6-MONTH MEDICARE SUPPLEMENT/ MEDIGAP OPEN ENROLLMENT PERIOD.

If you're considering dropping your Medicare Advantage plan and buying a Medicare Supplement plan,

BE CAREFUL.

Depending upon the rules of your particular state, you may have to go through medical underwriting to purchase a Medicare Supplement plan outside of a special window when you turn sixty-five. Medicare Supplement plans are *not* like Original Medicare Parts A and B, Medicare Part D, or Medicare Part C (Medicare Advantage plans) in that Medicare Supplement insurance companies *can* deny you coverage based on your health.

A Medicare Supplement policy is a separate policy from Original Medicare Parts A and B. Medicare Supplements are offered by Medicare Supplement insurance companies. These companies *can* deny you coverage or, at the very least, accept you but charge you a much higher premium. If you get denied coverage for a Medicare Supplement plan, you'll *only* have Original Medicare Parts A and B and a Medicare Part D Prescription Drug plan to fall back on, until the AEP (October 15-December 7th), when you can enroll in a Medicare Advantage plan once again. My advice is that if you want to go that way, you've got to apply and receive your acceptance or denial from the Medicare Supplement insurance company *before* you apply for Part D and drop your Medicare Advantage plan.

Re-read the prior paragraph. It's important.

In essence, you generally have a very small window to buy a Medicare Supplement plan with no medical questions to answer, and the Medicare Supplement insurance company must accept your enrollment. Said differently, Medicare Supplement plans have very narrow timeframes within which you can apply for coverage and not be subject to medical underwriting.

If you're on a Medicare Supplement already, be very, very sure you know what you're doing. Many people use a Medicare Supplement for a few years then move to a Medicare Advantage plan. Some people move from one Medicare Supplement plan to another to get a cheaper rate. **Whatever you do, don't drop a Medicare supplement plan before you get confirmation on your next insurance policy!**

If you drop or cancel a Medicare Supplement plan, odds are, it'll be tough to get back on to it. If you drop your Medicare Advantage plan and go back to Original Medicare Parts A and B and a Medicare Part D Prescription Drug Plan, do not automatically assume you'll be able to buy a Medicare Supplement plan. This is unlike Medicare Part D Prescription Drug Plans or Medicare Part C Medicare Advantage plans. Again, those types of plans must accept you with no medical underwriting.

That said, you better have a really good reason, and you better understand what benefits you will have in your new plan, as well as what you may be giving up, before switching plans—and from there, you can determine whether or not a change will truly be beneficial for you. The basic rule is this. *Don't* drop Medicare Advantage in favor of a Medicare Supplement plus a Medicare Part D Prescription Drug Plan *before* you get accepted to enroll in a Medicare Supplement plan, if that's what you're planning to do. If you're okay with moving away from a Medicare Advantage plan and going back to Original Medicare plus a Medicare Part D Prescription Drug Plan, you can do that during the OEP. If you want to change from your current Medicare Advantage plan and choose another one, you can do so—one time—during the OEP.

SECTION TWO NOTES

SECTION THREE: PREPARE TO PURCHASE

There are two ways to buy Medicare insurance.

1 Use a Medicare insurance agent

✓ Using a Medicare insurance agent doesn't cost you any more money, nor do you save money by buying a policy directly from an insurance company.

2 DIY (Do-It-Yourself)

Because it's the most common way folks buy Medicare insurance, this section is going to assist you for finding and meeting with a local, field-based Medicare insurance agent. You can also call a Hybrid Agency or navigate to their website to comparison shop online and over the phone. Head to prepareformedicare.com/links for a small list of those types of insurance agencies and agents

Earlier in the workbook, I outlined how to DIY buying a Medicare Part D Prescription Drug Plan on Medicare.gov. You certainly can DIY Medicare Supplement or Medicare Advantage enrollment, but if you'd like detailed DIY instructions, you'll have to buy the book! You can find those step-by-step directions and recommendations in Chapter Nine.

FIND AN AGENT

THE THREE TYPES OF MEDICARE INSURANCE AGENTS

There are three types of Medicare insurance agents—field-based agents, hybrid phone and web-assisted agents, and Medicare insurance company call center agents. Some agents specialize in Medicare Advantage, while others specialize and prefer Medicare Supplements. Ideally, you want one that specializes in Medicare Advantage, Medicare Part D Prescription Drug Plans, *and* Medicare Supplements. It's important to ask when you interview them, as I explain later.

1. FIELD-BASED AGENTS

These agents live in your local area and sell insurance by individually meeting with their potential and current customers. Often, they will come right to your house and review your options across the kitchen table. If you don't want them in your home, they'll meet you at a Starbucks, library, McDonald's—anywhere that's convenient for you. These appointments usually take an hour, sometimes longer, and sometimes require more than one sitting. Many agents have started doing meetings over Zoom or other videoconferencing as well.

The advantages of using a field-based agent are many. They usually know what Medicare insurance plans are available where you live, which companies are new, and which have been around for years. They know which companies are rolling out new and exciting plans, and which ones are on their way out of the area. These agents are normally hyper-connected to their local insurance company representatives and know what's going on with each company they represent.

They know which doctors and hospitals are in one company's network and not in others. They know which plan is hot that year and which plans are not. They know all of the particular state-based rules around Medicare Supplement insurance. They take pride in providing great customer support and service and often hand-hold their clients through many decisions.

Great field-based agents proactively reach out to you every fall to do an annual plan review with you to go over your existing coverage to see if it's still the right plan for you. They know when prescription drug formularies change, when prices go up, and when benefits go down. They make sure you get your ID cards when you buy a new policy. They're available via phone, almost 24/7. You might even get a birthday or holiday card from them. If you value having a local advocate helping you navigate the Medicare maze on your behalf, find a really good field-based agent. They can be invaluable.

There are two types of field-based Medicare insurance agents: Independent agents and Captive agents.

INDEPENDENT INSURANCE AGENTS

Independent agents are also known as multi-carrier agents, which, as the name suggests, are contracted to sell products for multiple Medicare insurance companies. They'll usually be able to sell a number of Medicare Supplement insurance companies, Medicare Part D Prescription Drug Plans, and Medicare Advantage plans. These agents usually work *with* an independent insurance agency, but not *for* an agency. It's a loose affiliation. In other words, the independent insurance agency doesn't technically employ the independent agent, but they may provide certain administrative services like contracting, customer service and scheduling help. In return, the independent agent aligns their Medicare insurance company contracts with the independent agency, and the agency makes a small commission every time the agent makes a sale.

Most independent insurance agents only represent three to seven companies, which means that not every agent can sell every product available to you. Most tend to make sure they're able to sell products from the large national or regional insurance companies like Mutual of Omaha, Aetna, United Healthcare, Humana, Cigna, Blue Cross and Blue Shield, and Centene/WellCare. However, there are lots of smaller Medicare insurance companies out there for which some agents don't bother to get contracted and licensed to sell. That doesn't mean they're not worthwhile to research; many of them offer fantastic products. It's again just important for you to understand that not every Medicare insurance agent sells products for every Medicare insurance company.

CAPTIVE INSURANCE AGENTS

Captive agents normally work for a Medicare insurance company and may only sell that company's products. For example, Humana employs quite a large captive sales force, and those agents may not sell United Healthcare or Aetna Medicare insurance policies, only Humana's.

There are some hybrids of this model; some insurance agencies do employ captive agents, but those agents *are* allowed to sell products from more than one Medicare insurance company—just not whichever company they want or choose, like the independent insurance agent can.

2. HYBRID AGENTS:

Online Insurance Agencies - Hybrid insurance agents, who use a combination of the telephone assisted by comparison tools found on websites to sell Medicare insurance, are very quickly gaining in popularity. Companies like eHealth, Select Quote, GoHealth, and many others employ thousands of captive insurance agents who can sell insurance over the phone. These companies are multi-carrier agencies, which means they sell people insurance policies from multiple Medicare insurance companies. These companies loosely fall under the emerging, Insurtech space which, in simple terms, utilizes real people on the telephone assisted by internet-based decision tools and even artificial intelligence to help people buy Medicare insurance policies.

3. INSURANCE COMPANY CALL CENTER AGENTS

Every Medicare insurance company either directly employs or contracts with third-party call centers to provide licensed insurance agents to take insurance applications over the phone. If you call a Medicare insurance company's toll-free number you found on a piece of mail you got in your mailbox, off of a TV ad, or a website, you'll be routed to these call centers.

These agents are considered captive as well and, as they're working for or on behalf of the Medicare insurance company, are *not* multi-carrier. They can only sell insurance for the company they are representing, so when you call them, they can't show Medicare insurance options from other companies.

There are generally two ways people find Medicare insurance agents.

1 Family, friends, neighbor referrals

2 Medicare insurance company referrals

If you've exhausted your network and still can't get a good referral, call a major Medicare health insurance company and ask them to connect you with one. Heck, ask them to connect you with three and interview all of them.

Interview them?

Yes.

A good agent can sell you an insurance policy. A *great* agent, an *expert*, is what you're looking for here. You should be looking for a Medicare insurance agent you can trust and rely on for a very long time because, ideally, he or she is helping you review your coverage annually and helping you with any customer service problems throughout the year when they arise.

You need to ask your potential Medicare insurance agent-for-life some very specific questions to make sure they are a contact person you'll want to keep on your team. A good agent can sell you an insurance policy. A *great* agent, an *expert*, is what you're looking for here. You should be looking for a Medicare insurance agent you can trust and rely on for a very long time because, ideally, he or she is helping you review your coverage annually and helping you with any customer service problems throughout the year when they arise.

Medicare insurance agents are a rare breed, but that doesn't mean 100% of them are *experts*. Just like everything in life, only a small percentage of Medicare insurance agents are top-notch experts in their field. Your goal is to find one of these great agents. You want to find a low-pressure, consultive salesperson who educates you and guides you through your needs, and helps you find the right fit. You're looking to weed out the high-pressure, move-fast salesperson who just wants to get in and get out of the appointment with a sale.

This is why, when the agent calls you, you call them, or the agent shows up in-person (only if you've invited them, of course), have some questions ready. My advice is to do this over the phone before setting up an in-person appointment. You may want to interview more than one agent until you find one who answers your questions to your satisfaction.

Remember, it's important to find a top-notch, experienced, knowledgeable, super-professional Medicare insurance agent you can count on for life.

Here are some questions you should ask your potential agent over the phone before scheduling any next steps or in-person appointments.

Are you ready? Okay, here's your Walter Cronkite moment!

1. How long have you been a Medicare insurance agent? (Needs to be over three years.)

yes ☐   no ☐

2. Do you consider yourself a full-time Medicare insurance agent? (Needs to be a yes.)

yes ☐   no ☐

3. Do you sell Medicare Advantage plans as well as Medicare Supplement plans? (Needs to be yes.)

yes ☐   no ☐

4. How many companies do you represent? (If you've chosen an Independent Agent, it needs to be a minimum of three, including a smattering of the big national ones—United Healthcare, Humana, Aetna, and Mutual of Omaha, for example. Captive agents usually only sell the company which employs them.)

_____

_____

_____

_____

5. Which Medicare insurance company products do you sell the most of and why? (Should be a good smattering of Medicare Supplements, Medicare Advantage plans, Medicare Part D Prescription Drug Plans, and some dental, vision, or other ancillary insurance products.)

_____

_____

_____

6. How many customers do you currently have? (Needs to be over 100.)

Over 100   Under 100
            ☐

7. Of those customers, how many are Medicare Advantage customers, and how many are Medicare Part D Prescription Drug Plan + Medicare Supplement customers? (Needs to be a nice balance between the two.)

_____

8. How many complaints from customers to the insurance company or Medicare have you been asked to respond to by the insurance company in the last twenty-four months? (Needs to be zero.)

Zero?

yes ☐   no ☐

9. Walk me through how you treat your customers when they buy a policy from you. (Needs to explain what they do immediately after you buy a policy, as well as when and how they review your coverage—should be at least once a year.)

_____

_____

_____

_____

10. How much commission do you make when you sell me a policy? (Needs to be specific and without much hesitation. Rates may vary depending They may pause when you ask, because not many people actually ask them this question! That's okay. But if they refuse to tell you or deflect, watch out and move on.)

Medicare Advantage:

_____

Medicare Part D Prescription Drug Plan:

_____

Medicare Supplement:

_____

That last question about commissions is going to be a touchy topic, probably for both you and your insurance agent. However, it's an important question to ask because the answer is going to give you some valuable insight into the psyche, professionalism, and forthrightness of your potential Medicare agent-for-life.

A professional, expert Medicare insurance agent won't have any issue at all telling you how much commission he or she stands to make when selling you a product. If an agent balks, then move on. Remember, independent Medicare insurance agents are just that—*independent*. That means they're independent contractors with no base salary, no benefits, no car allowance, and no gas money. They pay taxes on those commissions. Just like all of us, we work (or worked) and expect to receive compensation for our time, effort, expertise, and experience. The same holds true for independent Medicare insurance agents. The difference is, unlike a salaried employee, they only make money when they sell a policy. That money is paid to them by the Medicare insurance company, not you. That means *until you buy something from them, they're essentially working pro bono—for free.*

Ask them how much commission they're making if you enroll in the product they're selling. If they say they don't know or refuse to tell you, end the conversation right then and there. If your independent Medicare insurance agent won't disclose their commissions to you, what else are they not telling you?

In my opinion, you *want* a successful, highly paid Medicare insurance agent in your corner. You *want* them to be well-dressed and drive a premium automobile to your appointment or meeting. You *want* them to be proud to tell you how much commission they make. You *want* them to have hundreds of happy customers who have previously bought Medicare insurance with their help. You *want* them to be really, really good at what they do. After all, do you want to be associated with a poorly paid, poorly dressed, financially *unsuccessful* Medicare insurance agent as your agent-for-life? Not me!

If the insurance agent answers all of these questions to your satisfaction, now's the time to move ahead and set up a face-to-face sales appointment. Typically, this means the agent will come to your house or meet you at some other location, but it can also mean a Zoom meeting or other web-based videoconference. The meeting can also happen right over the phone. These meetings normally last anywhere between forty-five minutes to two hours, depending on the complexity of the Medicare insurance issues you're both trying to solve together.

If the insurance company didn't originally have you agree to a Scope of Appointment, the agent will do this now or in person when you meet.

Once you reach this stage—meeting with a Medicare insurance agent—it's generally time to buy something. That's what the insurance agent will expect you to do, and that's what you've prepared for! Sometimes it'll take a couple of meetings to get comfortable with the products and with each other. At the very least, you'll have a broader understanding of your options. You can always schedule a follow-up appointment if you need more time to think about it before you purchase a policy.

SECTION THREE NOTES

PREPARE FOR THE MEDICARE AGENT SALES APPOINTMENT

This section is meant to be used to help you organize your thoughts, coverage needs and how you currently or intend to use your Medicare insurance coverage. Completed, this will serve as a fantastic reference tool for you to use alongside or with your expert Medicare insurance agent!

It's also a handy reference tool if you're a DIY-er and shopping for Medicare insurance online or over the phone by yourself.

Remember, this is a reference tool for *you, the Medicare "consumer"* to you use – if filled out completely, it will contain personal health information you wouldn't necessarily want or need to share with a Medicare insurance company or agent. Medicare Advantage and Medicare Part D Prescription Drug Plan insurance companies cannot reject your application due to your health status or how many prescriptions you take. Medicare Supplement plans *may* be able to reject you, depending upon when you are trying to sign up and where you live.

Medicare insurance agents generally aren't allowed to ask you health-related questions that aren't on the policy applications. However, some of this information is very helpful for any Medicare insurance agent to know in order to help you find the best product for your Medicare insurance needs. It's going to be very difficult for an agent to help you find an insurance plan that covers your prescriptions if they don't know what prescriptions you need covered! In the end, it's up to you how much you share.

Which of the Three Options do you currently have or are exploring? (I've **bolded** what you'll have to actually buy or purchase from a Medicare insurance company.)

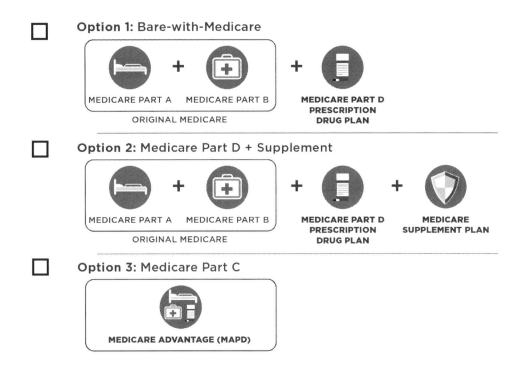

Circle your current or upcoming enrollment period:

AEP   OEP   IEP   SEP

If you haven't yet filled out the My Personal Medicare Information in the beginning of this workbook, you'll need to do that now. Your Medicare insurance agent will likely need much of that information.

Next, write down any doctors you've seen in the past or plan to see over the next twelve months. Hospitals and facilities, too.

_____

_____

_____

If you're a snowbird or if you travel often, write down where you plan to or routinely visit.

_____

_____

_____

Details of the plan you're currently on, as well as what you like and don't like about it. What you like about your plan.

_____

_____

_____

What you'd change about your plan if you could.

_____

_____

_____

Any additional benefits you would like, such as dental, vision, hearing, etc.

_____

_____

_____

Are you eligible for Medicare? Y/N

- o If yes, write down your Medicare number (found on your red, white, and blue Medicare card): _____

- o Are you still working?

  yes ☐   no ☐

Do you make more than approximately $20,000 per year as an individual or $26,000 as a couple?

  yes ☐   no ☐

Are you currently on Medicare?

  yes ☐   no ☐

If you haven't yet elected your Medicare insurance options or are new to Medicare, which Medicare path are you considering? (Circle one)

Option 1: Bare-with-Medicare

MEDICARE PART A   MEDICARE PART B   **MEDICARE PART D PRESCRIPTION DRUG PLAN**

ORIGINAL MEDICARE

Option 2: Medicare Part D + Supplement

MEDICARE PART A   MEDICARE PART B   **MEDICARE PART D PRESCRIPTION DRUG PLAN**   **MEDICARE SUPPLEMENT PLAN**

ORIGINAL MEDICARE

Option 3: Medicare Part C

MEDICARE ADVANTAGE (MAPD)

What kind of insurance coverage do you currently have? (Circle One)

Option 1: Bare-with-Medicare

Option 2: Medicare Part D + Supplement

Option 3: Medicare Part C

Group Medicare/Employer Retirement Plan

Still working and on my employer's health insurance plan

I have an Affordable Care Act plan

Other

Information about your other health coverage (if you have any), including policy and group numbers (found on your health insurance card).

Of the doctors you listed previously, are there any that are more important you must continue to be able to see?

_____

_____

_____

_____

_____

Are there any that are less important? **Circle** the doctors you would be willing to switch. What hospitals would you prefer to use if you need to?

_____

_____

_____

_____

_____

Are there any upcoming appointments or health care services you think you'll need in the next year or so?

_____

_____

_____

_____

_____

Do you wear glasses or use contacts?

yes ☐   no ☐

Do you have a hearing aid?

yes ☐   no ☐

Do you currently use any Durable Medical Equipment?

yes ☐   no ☐

Do you have dental insurance coverage? If so, list your dentist and coverage details.

_____

_____

_____

_____

_____

_____

Do you go to a gym?

yes ☐   no ☐

If so, which one? _____

What chronic conditions are you currently being treated for?

_____

_____

_____

_____

_____

_____

What can you afford in terms of a monthly premium? _____

★ ★ ★ ★ ★

We've reached the end of the Prepare for Medicare Workbook! Congratulations!

If you've read and completed it in its entirety, you've no doubt laid out a fine plan to shop, weigh options and purchase Medicare insurance based on your own personal healthcare and financial needs. Now is the time to buy Medicare insurance! The rest of the workbook contains space for you to enter additional helpful contact and planning information.

SECTION NOTES

SECTION NOTES

2021 — PART B PREMIUMS BY INCOME

The standard Part B premium amount in 2021 is $148.50. Most people pay the standard Part B premium amount. If your modified adjusted gross income as reported on your IRS tax return from 2 years ago is above a certain amount, you'll pay the standard premium amount and an Income Related Monthly Adjustment Amount (IRMAA). IRMAA is an extra charge added to your premium.

IF YOUR YEARLY INCOME IN 2019 (FOR WHAT YOU PAY IN 2021) WAS			
File individual tax return	File joint tax return	File married & separate tax return	You pay each month (in 2021)
$88,000 or less	$176,000 or less	$88,000 or less	$148.50
above $88,000 up to $111,000	above $176,000 up to $222,000	Not applicable	$207.90
above $111,000 up to $138,000	above $222,000 up to $276,000	Not applicable	$297.00
above $138,000 up to $165,000	above $276,000 up to $330,000	Not applicable	$386.10
above $165,000 and less than $500,000	above $330,000 and less than $750,000	above $88,000 and less than $412,000	$475.20
$500,000 or above	$750,000 and above	$412,000 and above	$504.90

2021   PART D PREMIUMS BY INCOME

The chart below shows your estimated prescription drug plan monthly premium based on your income as reported on your IRS tax return. If your income is above a certain limit, you'll pay an income-related monthly adjustment amount in addition to your plan premium.

The Income Related Monthly Adjustment Amounts (IRMAA) for Medicare Part B and D change annually. You can look for the most updated version prepareformedicare.com/links.

IF YOUR FILING STATUS AND YEARLY INCOME IN 2019 WAS			
FILE INDIVIDUAL TAX RETURN	FILE JOINT TAX RETURN	FILE MARRIED & SEPARATE TAX RETURN	YOU PAY EACH MONTH (IN 2021)
$88,000 or less	$176,000 or less	$88,000 or less	your plan premium
above $88,000 up to $111,000	above $176,000 up to $222,000	not applicable	$12.30 + your plan premium
above $111,000 up to $138,000	above $222,000 up to $276,000	not applicable	$31.80 + your plan premium
above $138,000 up to $165,000	above $276,000 up to $330,000	not applicable	$51.20 + your plan premium
above $165,000 and less than $500,000	above $330,000 and less than $750,000	above $88,000 and less than $412,000	$70.70 + your plan premium
$500,000 or above	$750,000 and above	$412,000 and above	$77.10 + your plan premium

ADDITIONAL CONTACTS

- Financial advisor(s):

  _____

  _____

  _____

  _____

  _____

- CPA or tax professionals:

  _____

  _____

  _____

  _____

  _____

- Medicare insurance agent

  _____

  _____

  _____

  _____

  _____

- Property and Casualty insurance agent

  _____

  _____

  _____

  _____

  _____

- Estate Planning contacts

  _____

  _____

  _____

  _____

  _____

- Banking information:

  _____

  _____

  _____

  _____

  _____

- Life insurance policies with up-to-date beneficiaries

  _____

  _____

  _____

  _____

  _____

- Long-term care insurance polices

  _____

  _____

  _____

  _____

- Children Names and phone numbers:

  _____

  _____

  _____

  _____

  _____

- Grandchildren Names and phone numbers (if applicable):

_____

_____

_____

_____

_____

ADDITIONAL CONTACT NOTES

ADDITIONAL NOTES

ADDITIONAL NOTES

ADDITIONAL NOTES

ADDITIONAL NOTES

ADDITIONAL NOTES

ADDITIONAL NOTES

ADDITIONAL NOTES

ADDITIONAL NOTES

ADDITIONAL NOTES

ADDITIONAL NOTES

ADDITIONAL NOTES

ADDITIONAL NOTES

ADDITIONAL NOTES

ADDITIONAL NOTES

ADDITIONAL NOTES

ADDITIONAL NOTES

ADDITIONAL NOTES

ADDITIONAL NOTES

ADDITIONAL NOTES

ADDITIONAL NOTES

ADDITIONAL NOTES

ADDITIONAL NOTES

ADDITIONAL NOTES

WHO IS MATT FERET?

Matt Feret began his professional career mowing lawns at age ten. He's surprised to have emerged many years later to find himself a Medicare insurance industry veteran, which *still* sounds weird in his head when he types it. He's made professional stops at Anthem, Humana, HCSC, CVS Health/Aetna and some he'd rather forget.

He is passionate about making it easy for people pick the right Medicare plan *for them* without the perceived requisite pain and suffering. Matt really likes talking about Medicare, personal finance, and retirement issues and feels happy when helping people understand them. He believes it's part of his purpose for being on the planet. The pursuit of laugher and happiness is one of his favorite pastimes.

Matt follows the Virginia Tech Hokies, likes attending obnoxiously loud heavy metal concerts, baseball games that go into extra innings and hiking. He'd bet you his 8th grade English teacher is floored he actually wrote a book. He also really loves his wife and kids who tolerate living with him in a suburb of Chicago. The family also includes two cats named Puck and Blossom which apparently are named after Shakespeare characters. His kids made him add their names to his bio.

Matt loves public and private speaking—come connect with him on the interwebs!

Company Name: MF Media, LLC

Email: mf@mattferet.com

Website: mattferet.com

LinkedIn: linkedin.com/in/mattferet

Twitter: @feret_matt

Facebook: https://www.facebook.com/mattferet/

Made in United States
Orlando, FL
12 March 2022

15710018R00059